Key Stage 1

Adding & Taking Away

Contents

Foreword..................................2	Addition: Money Problems..............26
How To Use This Book 3	Five More And Ten More 28
	Number Bonds To 100 30
Counting Numbers............................4	Estimating 32
Adding One More And Two More ..6	Subtraction: Money Problems........34
Number Lines 8	Five Less And Ten Less 36
Counting In Groups..........................10	Adding And Subtracting:
Counting In Patterns.......................12	Problems With Centimetres 38
Adding To Ten: Number Bonds 14	Important Numbers To Know 40
Numbers To 20.................................16	Writing Numbers In Words 42
Subtracting..18	Use Your Head! 44
One Less And Two Less 20	Answers 46
Bigger Numbers 22	
Doubling And Halving 24	**Check Your Progress! 48**

AUTHOR: Camilla de la Bédoyère
EDITORIAL: John Cattermole, Vicky Garrard, Julia Rolf
DESIGN: Jen Bishop, Dave Jones
ILLUSTRATORS: Bridget Dowty, Sarah Wimperis
PRODUCTION: Chris Herbert, Claire Walker

COMMISSIONING EDITOR: Polly Willis
PUBLISHER AND CREATIVE DIRECTOR: Nick Wells

3 book Pack ISBN 1-84451-085-9   Book ISBN 1-84451-018-2
6 book Pack ISBN 1-84451-089-1   Book ISBN 1-84451-091-3

First published in 2004

A copy of the CIP data for this book is available from the British Library upon request.

All rights reserved. No part of this publication may be reproduced, stored in a retrieval system, or transmitted in any form or by any means, without the prior written permission of the copyright holder.

Created and produced by
FLAME TREE PUBLISHING
Crabtree Hall,
Crabtree Lane,
Fulham, London SW6 6TY
United Kingdom
www.flametreepublishing.com

Flame Tree Publishing is part of The Foundry Creative Media Co. Ltd.

© The Foundry Creative Media Co. Ltd, 2004

Printed in Croatia

Foreword

Sometimes when I am crossing the playground on my way to visit a primary school I pass young children playing at schools. There is always a stern authoritarian little teacher at the front laying down the law to the unruly group of children in the pretend class. This puzzles me a little because the school I am visiting is very far from being like the children's play. Where do they get this Victorian view of what school is like? Perhaps it's handed down from generation to generation through the genes. Certainly they don't get it from their primary school. Teachers today are more often found alongside their pupils, who are learning by actually doing things for themselves, rather than merely listening and obeying instructions.

Busy children, interested and involved in their classroom reflect what we know about how they learn. Of course they learn from teachers but most of all they learn from their experience of life and their life is spent both in and out of school. Indeed, if we compare the impact upon children of even the finest schools and teachers, we find that three or four times as great an impact is made by the reality of children's lives outside the school. That reality has the parent at the all important centre. No adult can have so much impact, for good or ill, as the young child's mother or father.

This book, and others in the series, are founded on the sure belief that the great majority of parents want to help their children grow and learn and that teachers are keen to support them. The days when parents were kept at arm's length from schools are long gone and over the years we have moved well beyond the white line painted on the playground across which no parent must pass without an appointment. Now parents move freely in and out of schools and very often are found in the classrooms backing up the teachers. Both sides of the partnership know how important it is that children should be challenged and stimulated both in and out of school.

Perhaps the most vital part of this book is where parents and children are encouraged to develop activities beyond those offered on the page. The more the children explore and use the ideas and techniques we want them to learn, the more they will make new knowledge of their very own. It's not just getting the right answer, it's growing as a person through gaining skill in action and not only in books. The best way to learn is to live.

I remember reading a story to a group of nine year old boys. The story was about soldiers and of course the boys, bloodthirsty as ever, were hanging on my every word. I came to the word khaki and I asked the group "What colour is khaki?" One boy was quick to answer. "Silver" he said, "It's silver." "Silver? I queried. "Yes," he said with absolute confidence, "silver, my Dad's car key is silver." Now I reckon I'm a pretty good teller of stories to children but when it came down to it, all my dramatic reading of a gripping story gave way immediately to the power of the boy's experience of life. That meant so much more to him, as it does to all children.

JOHN COE
General Secretary, National Association for Primary Education (NAPE).

Parents and teachers work together in NAPE to improve the quality of learning and teaching in primary schools. We campaign hard for a better deal for children at the vital early stage of their education upon which later success depends. We are always pleased to hear from parents.

NAPE, Moulton College, Moulton, Northampton, NN3 7RR,
Telephone: 01604 647 646 Web: www. nape.org.uk

How To Use This Book

Adding & Taking Away is one of six books in the **Revision, Practice & Home Learning** series for Key Stage One. These books have been devised to help you support your child as they approach the end of Key Stage One, in Year Two. Many children will be required to undergo assessment in preparation for their move to Key Stage Two.

The book follows key topics of the National Numeracy Strategy and it aims to set out the key skills covered at school. Your child can revise each topic then practise the skills by completing the questions. You should go through the book together; your child will need you on hand to guide them through each subject. There are **Activity** boxes which give your child activities or investigations to carry out once the book has been put away.

You will also find **Parents Start Here** boxes to give you extra information and guidance.

Before you begin any learning session with the book, ensure your child is relaxed and comfortable.

- Ensure they are sitting comfortably.
- Encourage a good writing grip and neat presentation.
- Give your child access to water; research suggests that children who drink water when they work are able to perform better.
- Keep a Maths Kit to hand: this can be an old shoebox containing a jar of counters, dice, pack of cards, ruler, measuring tape, grid paper, spent matches, building cubes, pencils, scissors, paper and a calculator.

Do not attempt to complete too many pages in one sitting; children have short attention spans and you want the experience to remain pleasurable. Offer your child plenty of praise for the work they accomplish. Revising is most effective if completed in short chunks. Topics should be revisited regularly to develop long-term memory patterns; your child is revising these topics for life, not just exams.

There is a checklist at the end of the book; you can use this to show your child how they are progressing. You could introduce a reward system too; children benefit enormously from rewards and praise.

Most importantly, the time you spend together with this book should be enjoyable for both of you.

KS1: Adding & Taking Away

Top Tip! Remember to give your child lots of praise – they will work so much better.

Parents Start Here...

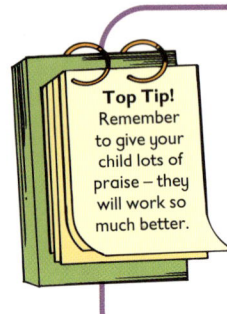

Help your child identify number patterns in the Number Square. If they find the questions on these pages easy, challenge them to use the Square to do some more difficult additions.

Counting Numbers

Remember!

- Use a pencil to write numbers.
- Write numbers clearly.
- You can use a Number Square to help you count.

1	2	3	4	5	6	7	8	9	10
11	12	13	14	15	16	17	18	19	20
21	22	23	24	25	26	27	28	29	30
31	32	33	34	35	36	37	38	39	40
41	42	43	44	45	46	47	48	49	50
51	52	53	54	55	56	57	58	59	60
61	62	63	64	65	66	67	68	69	70
71	72	73	74	75	76	77	78	79	80
81	82	83	84	85	86	87	88	89	90
91	92	93	94	95	96	97	98	99	100

Use this Number Square to answer the questions. Find the number and count forwards to find the answer.

Counting Numbers

1. What number comes after **75**? 76

2. Fill in the missing numbers:

23 24 25 26 **27 28** 29 **30**

3. Write down any three numbers that end in a zero (0):

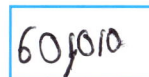

10000   11320   60,010

4. What number comes between **16** and **18**? 17

TRY THIS

Activity

Find out the names of the largest animal, tallest tree and the highest mountain in the world.

Something To Make

Why don't you have go at making your own Number Square? Find a big piece of card or stiff paper (the back of an empty cereal box would be perfect, but always ask a grown-up to help you if you are using scissors). Count the number of boxes there are in the Number Square on page 4 and, using a pencil and ruler, carefully draw a grid onto your piece of card. When you are sure you have got it just right, use your best handwriting to fill in the numbers. You may want to write the odd numbers in one colour and the even numbers in another.

Check Your Progress!
Counting Numbers
Turn to page 48 and put a tick next to what you have just learned.

KS1: Adding & Taking Away

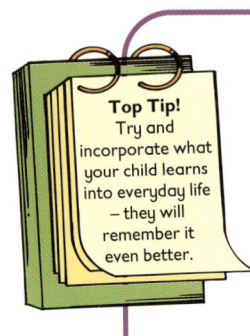

Top Tip! Try and incorporate what your child learns into everyday life – they will remember it even better.

Parents Start Here...

While the problems on these pages are simple, it is worth ensuring your child can do them before they develop the concept of 'more than' in Key Stage Two. It is also good for a child's confidence to complete a page of problems with ease.

Adding One More And Two More

Remember!

- Adding 1 is the same as having 1 more.
- Adding 2 is the same as having 2 more.
- You can add 1 more or 2 more to any number you like.
- Use the Number Square to add 1 more or 2 more.

1. Draw **1** more smiley face:

How many are there now? **4**

2. Draw **2** more sweets:

How many are there now? **3**

6

Adding One More And Two More

3. How many lollies are there altogether?

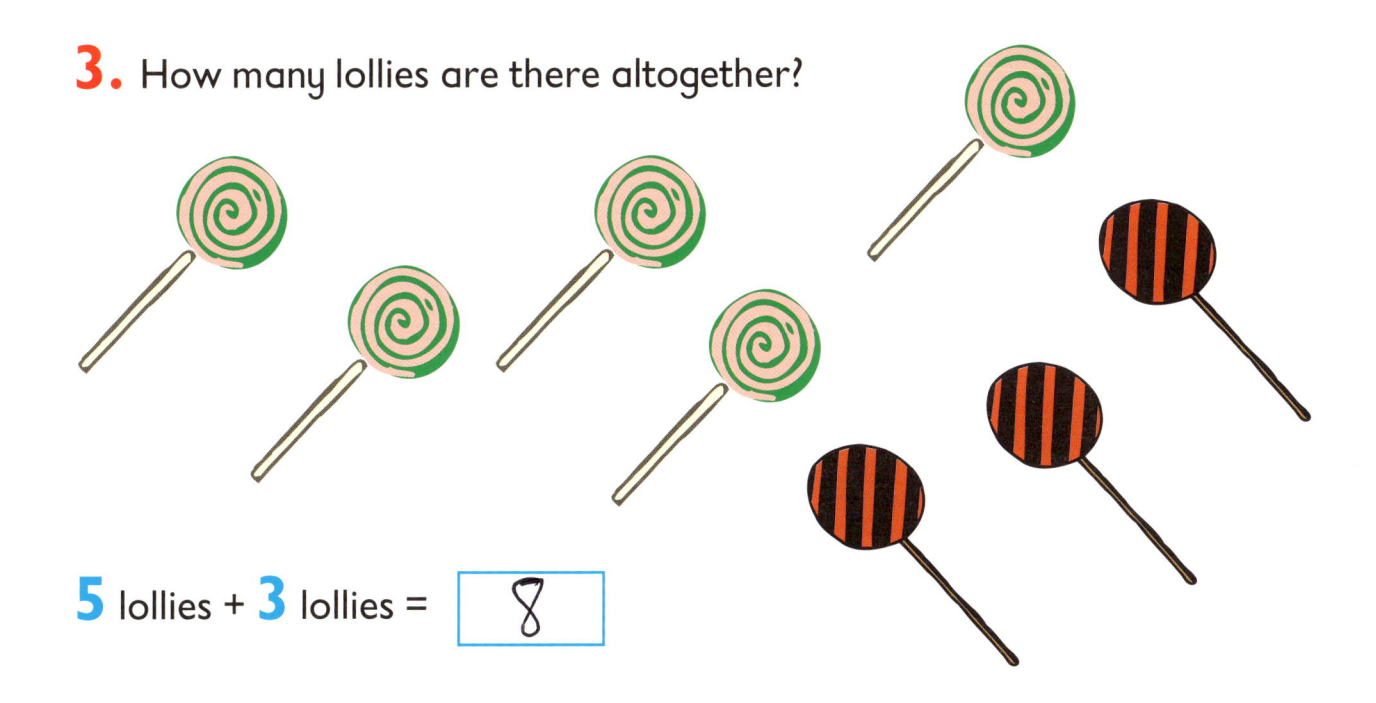

5 lollies + **3** lollies = ☐ 8

4. a) How many dots are there altogether?

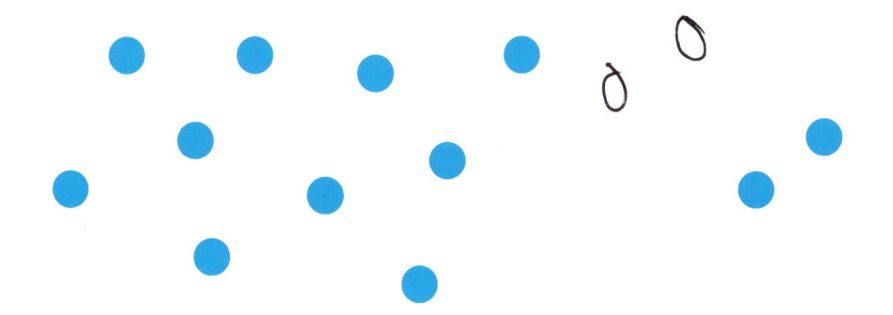

(two handwritten circles drawn)

b) Draw **2** more dots. How many dots are there now? ☐ 14

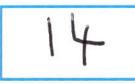

Activity
TRY THIS

Next time your Mum or Dad gives you a treat, try asking for 'just one more' and see if you are lucky!

Check Your Progress!
Adding One More And Two More ☐
Turn to page 48 and put a tick next to what you have just learned.

KS1: Adding & Taking Away

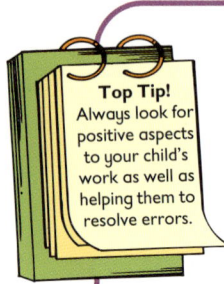

Parents Start Here...

Top Tip! Always look for positive aspects to your child's work as well as helping them to resolve errors.

Encourage your child to draw their own number line to answer question 5. Remind them to draw 'bouncing arrows' when they use number lines to add.

Number Lines

Remember!

- Use a number line to help you add.
- Numbers can be odd or even.
- Even numbers end in 0, 2 4, 6 or 8.

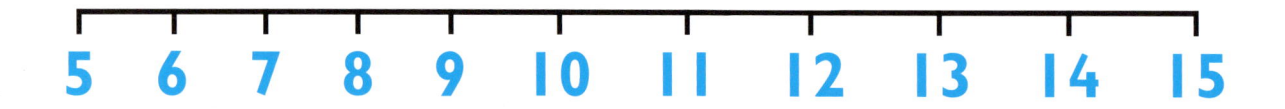

5 6 7 8 9 10 11 12 13 14 15

Use the number line to answer these questions:

1. Write in the missing numbers:

6   7   [8]   9   10   [11]   12

2. Add 2 to each of these numbers:

a) 5 + 2 = [7]

b) 8 + 2 = [10]

c) 13 + 2 = [15]

8

Number Lines

3. Add **3** to each of these numbers:

a) 5 + 3 = 8

b) 8 + 3 = 11

c) 13 + 3 = 16

4. Circle the even numbers:

1 ② 3 ④ 5 ⑥ 7 ⑧ 9 ⑩ 11 ⑫

5. Write these odd numbers out in order, from smallest to largest:

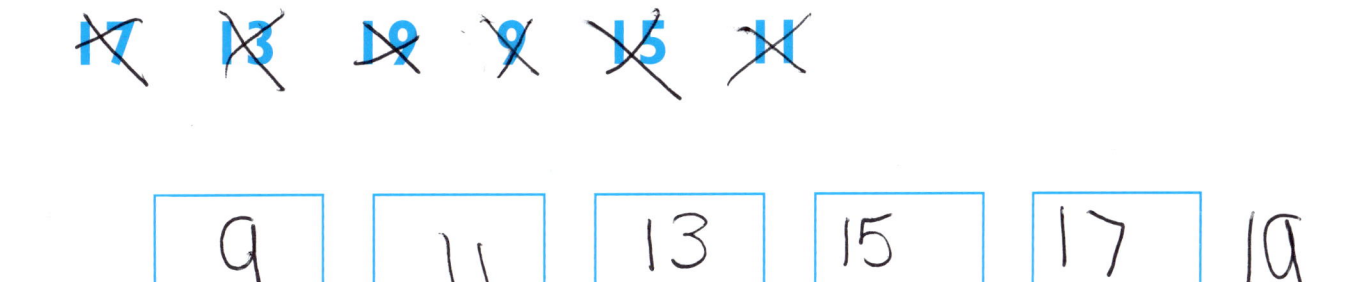

~~17~~ ~~13~~ ~~19~~ ~~9~~ ~~15~~ ~~11~~

| 9 | 11 | 13 | 15 | 17 | 19 |

Activity

TRY THIS

Draw your own Number Square (like the one on Page 4) and colour in all the boxes with even numbers. Can you see a pattern?

Check Your Progress!
Number Lines
Turn to page 48 and put a tick next to what you have just learned.

9

KS1: Adding & Taking Away

Top Tip! If your child loses concentration here, let them take a break.

Parents Start Here...

Using buttons, counters or coins ask your child to make groups of 2, then groups of 3, etc. Children need to see numbers at work in a practical way; keep a pot of counters at hand so they can turn any written calculation in to a practical task.

Counting In Groups

Remember!

- Counting in groups is quick and easy.
- A pair is a group of 2.
- Count each group carefully.

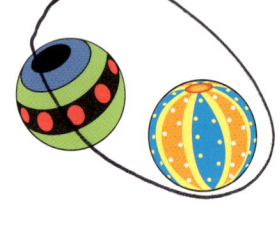

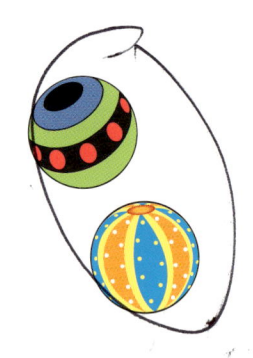

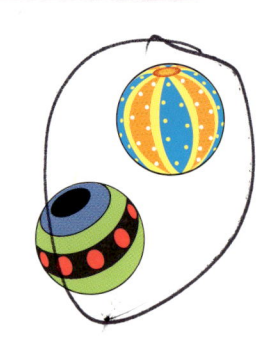

1. Draw a ring around each group of **2**:

How many balls are there altogether? [8]

2. Draw a ring around each group of **3**:

How many daisies are there altogether? [9]

Counting In Groups

3. Draw **5** balloons in each square:

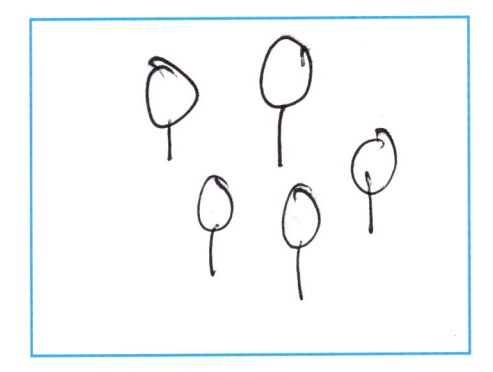

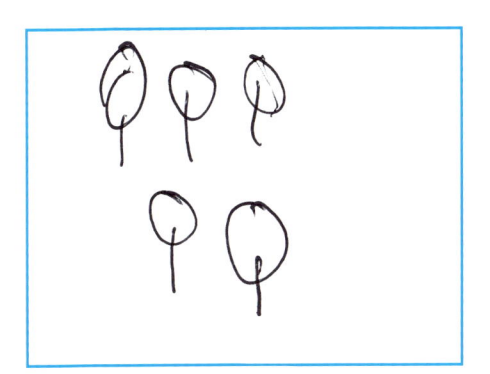

How many balloons have you drawn altogether? 10

4. Look at the groups of dots then complete the sentences below:

There are 3 groups of dots.

Each group has 4 dots in it.

Activity

Shoes are made in pairs. Find out how many shoes you have and how many pairs of shoes you have. Who has the most shoes in your family?

I have ☐ shoes.

I have ☐ pairs of shoes.

Check Your Progress!
Counting In Groups
Turn to page 48 and put a tick next to what you have just learned.

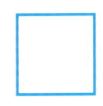

KS1: Adding & Taking Away

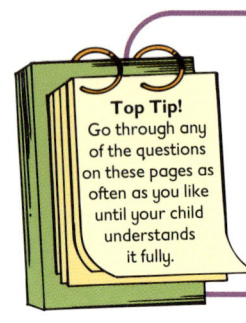

Top Tip! Go through any of the questions on these pages as often as you like until your child understands it fully.

Parents Start Here...

Playing dominoes and board games with dice can help your child count in groups and visualise numbers.

Counting In Patterns

Remember!
- Numbers can make patterns.
- Patterns help us to add or subtract numbers.
- A sequence of numbers is a list of numbers that make a pattern.

Look at these sequences of numbers and think about the gaps between each number. Use the sequences to answer the questions.

1. 2   4   6   8   10   12

a) What number has been added each time?   **2**

b) Tick the correct sentence:

These numbers are all odd.   ☐

These numbers are all even.   ✓

12

Counting In Patterns

2.   3   6   9   12   15

a) What number has been added each time?   3

b) What is the next number in this sequence?   18

3.   10   15   20   25   30

a) What number has been added each time?   5

b) What number would come before 10 in this sequence?   5

4. Use the Number Square at the beginning of your book to write your own number sequence of 5 numbers, starting at number 4 and adding 4 each time:

4   8   12   16   20

TRY THIS — Activity

Make your own giant number line with pieces of paper or using a chalk line drawn on the pavement. See if you can jump in groups of 2 or 3.

Check Your Progress!
Counting In Patterns
Turn to page 48 and put a tick next to what you have just learned.

KS1: Adding & Taking Away

Top Tip! If your child struggles with anything, don't worry – let them go at their own pace.

Parents Start Here...

Learning important number bonds will make your child's journey through the curriculum much easier. Mental arithmetic is an essential part of the Numeracy Strategy and number bonds are the foundation for mental maths.

Adding To Ten: Number Bonds

Remember!
- There are many ways you can add to 10.
- These are called number bonds.
- Learn the number bonds off by heart.

Use this number line to help you complete the questions.

1 2 3 4 5 6 7 8 9 10

1. Billy has **5** mice. How many more mice does he need to make **10**?

5

14

Adding To Ten: Number Bonds

2. Here are **8** dots. Draw in more dots so there are **10** altogether:

• • • • ○
• • • • ○

How many dots did you draw? **2**

3. Sox the Squirrel has **4** acorns but he needs **10**.

How many more acorns does Sox have to find? **6**

4. Fill in the boxes:

7 + **3** = 10   10 **+** 0 = 10

9 + 1 = 10   2 + **8** = 10

4 + 6 = **10**   5 + 5 = **10**

Activity

TRY THIS

Learn your number bonds off by heart. Once you know them you'll never forget them and they will help you do all sorts of sums in your head.

Check Your Progress!
Adding To Ten: Number Bonds
Turn to page 48 and put a tick next to what you have just learned.

KS1: Adding & Taking Away

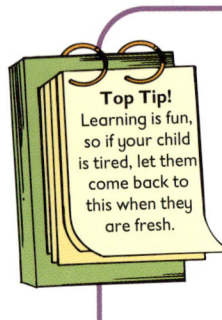

Top Tip! Learning is fun, so if your child is tired, let them come back to this when they are fresh.

Parents Start Here...

Develop the concept of number bonds further: ask your child if they can think of different ways to make the number 12, or 15, for example. Repeat the sums over and over so that your child commits them to memory.

Numbers To 20

Remember!

- There are many ways you can add to 20.
- These are called number bonds.
- Learn these number bonds off by heart.

Here are 2 ways to make 20:

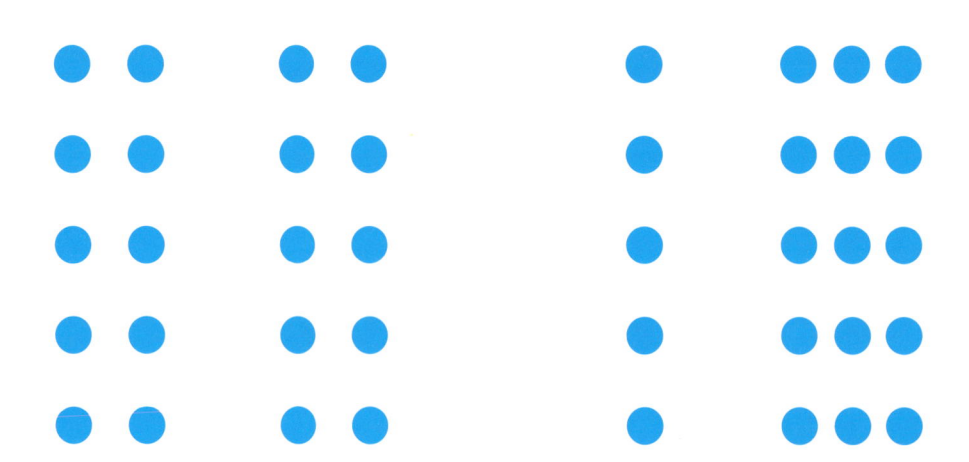

10 + 10 = 20   5 + 15 = 20

Numbers To 20

Complete these sums. Draw dots if it helps you, or you can use your Number Square.

2 + [18] = 20

7 + [13] = 20

[7] + 13 = 20

9 + 11 = [20]

1 + [~~20~~ 19] = 20

20 + [0] = 20

[17] + 3 = 20

16 + [4] = 20

15 + [5] = 20

17 + [3] = 20

[2~~4~~] + 18 = 20

[1] + 19 = 20

2 + [18] = 20

4 + [16] = 20

5 + 15 = [20]

6 + [14] = 20

[12] + 8 = 20

10 + [10] = 20

Activity
TRY THIS

Ask a grown-up to find you 20 1p coins and lay them out on a table. See how many ways you can group them to make 20. You should be able to find lots.

Check Your Progress!
Numbers To 20 [ ]
Turn to page 48 and put a tick next to what you have just learned.

KS1: Adding & Taking Away

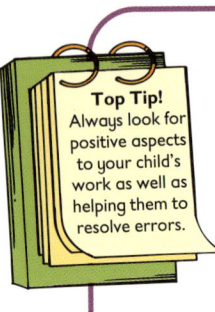

Top Tip! Always look for positive aspects to your child's work as well as helping them to resolve errors.

Parents Start Here...

Ensure your child has understood that adding and subtracting are opposites and are connected. Use your counters to show how you can add 5 counters then take them away again to get your original number.

Subtracting

Remember!

- When you take away you make a number smaller.
- Taking away and subtracting are the same thing.
- Adding and subtracting are the opposite.
- When you use a number line to subtract, the bouncing arrows go backwards.

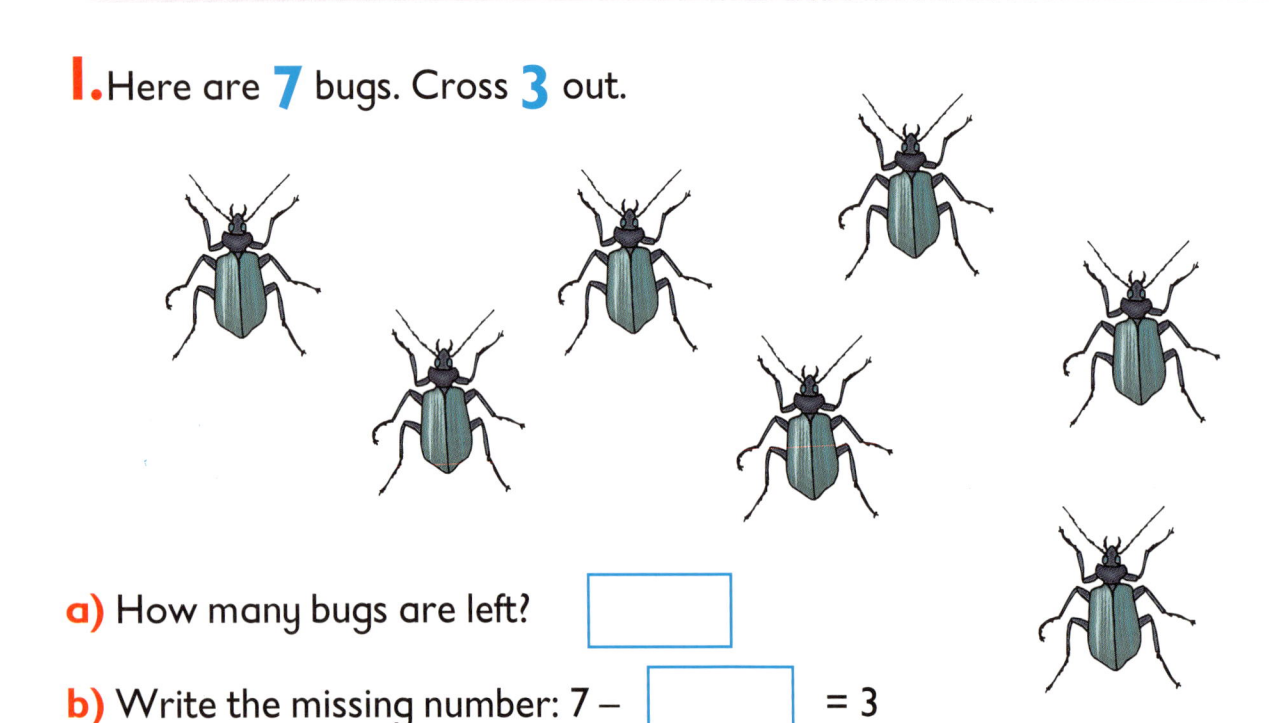

1. Here are **7** bugs. Cross **3** out.

a) How many bugs are left? ☐

b) Write the missing number: 7 − ☐ = 3

Subtracting

2. Use this number line to answer the questions. Remember to draw bouncing arrows backwards.

0 1 2 3 4 5 6 7 8 9 10

a) 10 − 1 = ☐

b) 8 − 2 = ☐

c) 5 − 5 = ☐

3. If you know your number bonds to 10 you will find these calculations easy:

a) 10 − 5 = ☐   d) 10 − 3 = ☐

b) 10 − 6 = ☐   e) 10 − 1 = ☐

c) 10 − 2 = ☐

TRY THIS

Activity

Think of a number between 0 and 10. Add 5 to it. Now take away 3. Now add 4. Take away 2. Take away the number you originally thought of. You will be left with 4. Magic!!

Check Your Progress!

Subtracting ☐

Turn to page 48 and put a tick next to what you have just learned.

KS1: Adding & Taking Away

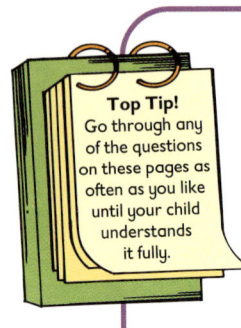

Parents Start Here...

Top Tip! Go through any of the questions on these pages as often as you like until your child understands it fully.

If your child has understood the ordering of numbers correctly they will be able to do the calculations on these pages without recourse to their fingers, a number line or Number Square. If they struggle you can practise some more simple questions like these together.

One Less And Two Less

Remember!

- Subtracting 1 is the same as having 1 less.
- Subtracting 2 is the same as having 2 less.

Try to do these questions in your head.

Only use a number line or your Number Square if you are really stuck.

1. a) 15 is 1 less than ☐

b) 99 is 1 less than ☐

c) 34 is 2 less than ☐

d) 78 is 2 less than ☐

e) 59 is 1 less than ☐

One Less And Two Less

2. a) 75 – 2 = ☐

b) 13 – ☐ = 12

c) 40 – 2 = ☐

d) 28 – ☐ = 26

e) 88 – 2 = ☐

3. a) Difference means subtract or minus. Use your Number Square to help.

The difference between **5** and **6** is **1**

a) the difference between 5 and 7 is ☐

b) the difference between 17 and 19 is ☐

c) the difference between 23 and 25 is ☐

d) the difference between 92 and 93 is ☐

TRY THIS **Activity**

Find out the number that is one less than 1000. You could try this on a calculator if you like.

Check Your Progress!
One Less And Two Less ☐
Turn to page 48 and put a tick next to what you have just learned.

21

KS1: Adding & Taking Away

Top Tip! Remember to give your child lots of praise – they will work so much better.

Parents Start Here...

Some children are ready to learn larger numbers earlier than others; you need to make that judgement yourself. Your child may find numbers fascinating, and be ready to learn about thousands, tens of thousands and millions.

Bigger Numbers

Remember!

- Use your Number Square to find bigger numbers.
- Numbers go on forever.
- It is important to write big numbers clearly.

1. Fill in the missing numbers in these sequences.

Finding the number patterns will help you:

a) 10 20 ☐ 40 ☐ 60 70 ☐ ☐ 100

b) 35 45 ☐ 65 ☐ 85 95

c) 13 23 ☐ 43 ☐ 63 73 ☐

d) 19 ☐ 39 ☐ 59 ☐ ☐

e) 100 200 300 ☐ 500 ☐ 700 800 ☐ 1000

22

Bigger Numbers

2. Copy out these numbers, putting them in the right order, smallest first.

a)   1000   10   100   0

b)   75   5   91   4   50

c)   82   75   88   91   74

3. An estimate is a good guess.

Here are two jars of sweets. Estimate how many sweets you think there might be in each jar. Do not count them.

A

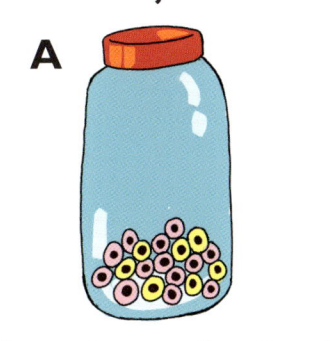

B

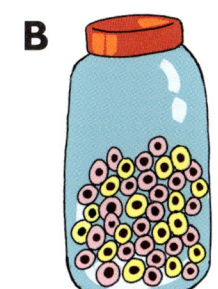

My estimate for Jar A ☐   My estimate for Jar B ☐

TRY THIS

Activity

Use a calculator to practise making some big numbers. What is the largest number you can make on your calculator? Ask a grown-up to help you.

Check Your Progress! ☐
Bigger Numbers
Turn to page 48 and put a tick next to what you have just learned.

KS1: Adding & Taking Away

Top Tip! If your child struggles with anything, don't worry – let them go at their own pace.

Parents Start Here...

When children learn how to carry out more complicated addition and subtraction sums in their heads, they are taught how to use the doubling and halving technique. It is useful to be accustomed to this practice from an early stage.

Doubling And Halving

Remember!

- When you *double* a number it gets bigger – Double 5 is 10.
- When you *halve* a number it gets smaller – Half of 10 is 5.
- Doubling and halving are *opposites*.

1. Errol drinks **2** glasses of water, but his sister Fran drinks double that number.

How many glasses of water does Fran drink? ☐

2. Jacob made **4** red jellies but made double the number of green jellies.

a) How many green jellies did Jacob make? ☐

b) How many jellies did Jacob make altogether? ☐

24

Doubling And Halving

3. Tick the correct answer:

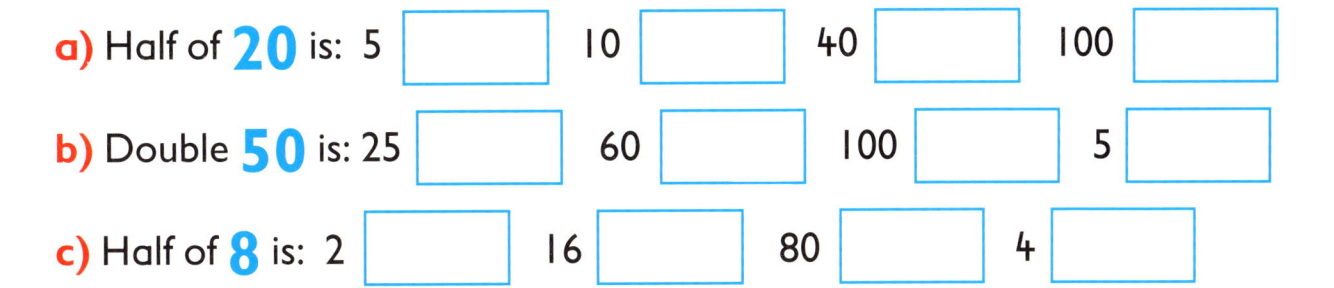

a) Half of **20** is: 5 ☐   10 ☐   40 ☐   100 ☐

b) Double **50** is: 25 ☐   60 ☐   100 ☐   5 ☐

c) Half of **8** is: 2 ☐   16 ☐   80 ☐   4 ☐

4. Match the number to its half. One has been done for you:

20	4
8	50
14	7
100	3
6	10

(6 → 3 has been matched)

Activity

TRY THIS

When you go shopping ask your Mum or Dad if you can help weigh out some fruit or vegetables. See if you can double and halve the amounts you have weighed.

Check Your Progress! ☐
Doubling And Halving ☐
Turn to page 48 and put a tick next to what you have just learned.

KS1: Adding & Taking Away

Top Tip! If your child loses concentration here, let them take a break.

Parents Start Here...

Ensure your child recognises all the coins and their values.

Addition: Money Problems

Remember!

- There are 100 pence (p) in a pound (£).
- You need to use the symbols p and £ when writing money calculations.
- When you add money start with the highest value coin (the one that is worth most).
- You can use the Number Square to solve money problems.

this is a pound sign — £5.89

this is a decimal point – it keeps the £ and p apart

you do not need the pence sign (p) when you have the pound sign

1. How much is this altogether? ☐

20p   10p   2p

26

Addition: Money Problems

2. Angela bought a chewy sweet for 12p.

She gave the shop-keeper a 20p coin.

How much change did Angela get? ☐

3. Tarik used 3 coins that were all the same to buy an apple.

The apple cost 30p.

Draw the coins that Tarik used:

4. a) Jenny gets 50p pocket money from her Mum and 50p from her Dad.

How much money does Jenny have? ☐

b) Jenny visits her Granny, who gives her a one pound coin.

Now how much money does Jenny have altogether? ☐

TRY THIS

Activity

Ask a grown-up to help you make coin rubbings. You will need thin white paper, crayons and lots of different coins.

Check Your Progress!
Addition: Money Problems ☐
Turn to page 48 and put a tick next to what you have just learned.

KS1: Adding & Taking Away

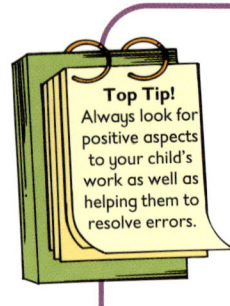

Top Tip! Always look for positive aspects to your child's work as well as helping them to resolve errors.

Parents Start Here...

Adding in 5s and 10s is easy once your child has recognised the pattern. Use 5p and 10p coins to help your child count in these groups.

Five More And Ten More

Remember!

- When you count in fives the answer will end in 5 or 0.
- When you count in tens the answer will end in 0.
- You can add 5 or 10 to any number you like.

1. Look at the Number Square and find all the numbers that end in **5** or **0**.

Write them in order in to these boxes. Write the smallest first.

2. Colour in all the boxes that have numbers ending in **0**.

Have you coloured in half of the boxes?

Yes ☐

No ☐

28

Five More And Ten More

3. Complete these sums.

You can use the Number Square, or your fingers, to help you:

a) 12 + 5 = ☐

b) 23 + 10 = ☐

c) 33 + 5 = ☐

d) 72 + 5 = ☐

e) 61 + 10 = ☐

f) 1 + 10 = ☐

g) 40 + ☐ = 45

h) 40 + ☐ = 50

4. Can you do this sum? You can add **10** first, then add **5**:

10 + 15 = ☐

TRY THIS Activity

Choose any number between 0 and 10, but not 5. Now add on 5. Keep on adding 5 and see how far you can go. Do not write the numbers down; this is a game to play in your head.

Check Your Progress!
Five More And Ten More ☐
Turn to page 48 and put a tick next to what you have just learned.

KS1: Adding & Taking Away

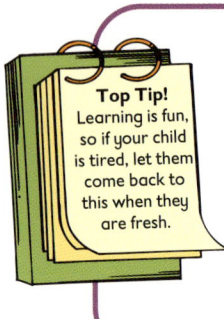

Top Tip! Learning is fun, so if your child is tired, let them come back to this when they are fresh.

Parents Start Here...

Show your child how the number bonds to 100 are mostly very similar to the number bonds to 10. If your child has found this concept easy challenge them to think of number bonds to 1000.

Number Bonds To 100

Remember!

- There are different ways to make 100.
- These are called number bonds.
- Learning number bonds helps you add and subtract.

Use your Number Square or this number line to help you complete the questions:

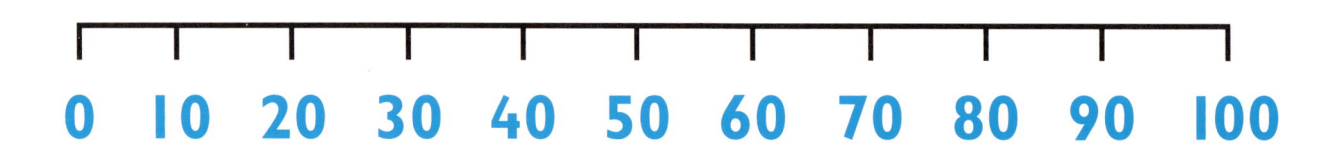

0 10 20 30 40 50 60 70 80 90 100

1. Farmer Jill has **50** sheep but she wants **100** sheep.

How many more sheep should Farmer Jill buy at market? ☐

30

Number Bonds To 100

2. Cecil the Centipede has **100** legs. He has **20** red socks. All the rest of his socks are blue.

How many blue socks does Cecil have? ☐

3.
a) 10 + ☐ = 100

b) 60 + ☐ = 100

c) ☐ + 70 = 100

d) ☐ + 20 = 100

e) 50 + ☐ = 100

f) 80 + ☐ = 100

g) 30 + ☐ = 100

h) ☐ + 40 = 100

i) ☐ + 90 = 100

TRY THIS — Activity

Ask a grown-up to find you a tape measure or metre rule. You will see that one metre is divided into 100 centimetres. Every 10 centimetres is marked, so you can count in 10s.

Check Your Progress!
Number Bonds To 100 ☐
Turn to page 48 and put a tick next to what you have just learned.

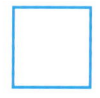

KS1: Adding & Taking Away

Top Tip! Try and incorporate what your child learns into everyday life – they will remember it even better.

Parents Start Here...

Children learn to estimate in order to assess whether they have got the correct answer or not. Estimating encourages children to think about the problem before they attempt to solve it.

Estimating

Remember!

- A good guess is called an estimate.
- You can estimate an answer before you do a sum.
- Sometimes an estimate is enough.
- An estimate is never wrong, though it could be a bad estimate.

1. Estimate how many dots you can see.

My estimate: ☐   Count the dots: ☐

What is the difference between your estimate and the real number? ☐

Do you think your estimate was good or bad? ☐

Estimating

2. Draw a dot where you think the centre of the circle is:

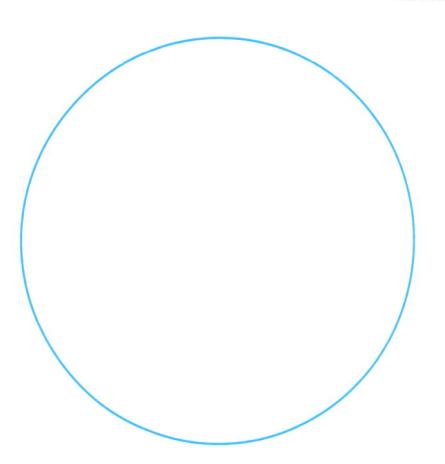

3. Estimate how many books are on this bookshelf. Have a look, but don't count!

Estimate: ☐   Now count the books: ☐

What was the difference between
your estimate and the real number? ☐

Do you think your estimate was good or bad? ☐

TRY THIS

Activity

Ask a grown-up to time you when you brush your teeth tonight. Estimate how long you spent brushing them, then see how close you were to the actual time.

Check Your Progress!

Estimating ☐

Turn to page 48 and put a tick next to what you have just learned.

KS1: Adding & Taking Away

Top Tip! Go through any of the questions on these pages as often as you like until your child understands it fully.

Parents Start Here...

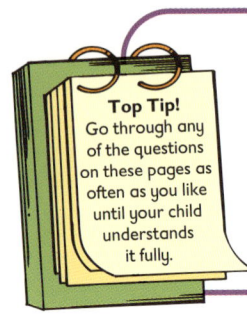

Help your child do the calculations on these pages by providing them with real money to play with.

Subtraction: Money Problems

Remember!

- There are 100 pence (p) in a pound (£).
- You must use the symbols for pounds £ and pence p.
- You can use the Number Square to solve money problems.

1. This is Mohammed's pocket money.

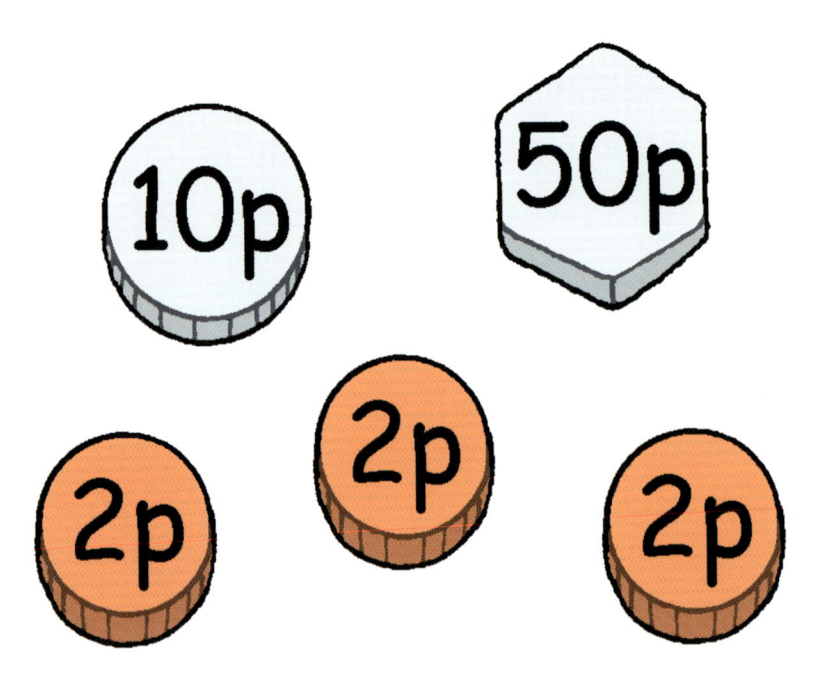

10p   50p

2p   2p   2p

If he loses 12p, how much will he have left?

34

Subtraction: Money Problems

2. Complete these money questions.

You can use your Number Square to help.

a) 75p – 10p = ☐

b) £1.00 – 50p = ☐

c) 10p – 5p = ☐

3. Jack and Jill's plastic bucket cost 60p.

How much change do they get from £1.00? ☐

4. Mary's little lamb cost £2.50.

How much change did she get from £3.00? ☐

5. The Queen of Hearts sold 10 jam tarts to the Jack of Hearts.

They cost 2p each.

The Jack of Hearts paid with two 10p coins.

Did the Queen give the Jack any change?

Yes ☐   No ☐

TRY THIS

Activity

Ask your Mum or Dad if you can help them pay for their shopping. See if you can work out the change they are owed.

Check Your Progress!
Subtraction: Money Problems ☐
Turn to page 48 and put a tick next to what you have just learned.

KS1: Adding & Taking Away

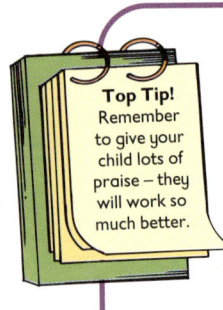

Top Tip! Remember to give your child lots of praise – they will work so much better.

Parents Start Here...

Ask your child to take 10 away from any number on the Number Square so they can identify the pattern. Recognising number patterns helps children understand the relationship between numbers and generates more interest in the subject.

Five Less And Ten Less

Remember!

- When you take away 5 you have 5 less.
- When you take away 10 you have 10 less.
- Subtracting 5 is the opposite of adding 5.
- Subtracting 10 is the opposite of adding 10.

Use your Number Square to help you complete these questions.

1. Colour in the correct answers:

15 – 5 = 9	29 – 5 = 24	99 – 10 = 89	17 – 5 = 13
36 – 10 = 25	71 – 5 = 66	13 – 10 = 12	40 – 5 = 35
22 – 10 = 12	5 – 5 = 1	85 – 5 = 79	76 – 5 = 71

Five Less And Ten Less

2. a) 65 – 5 = ☐   e) 99 – 10 = ☐

b) 100 – 10 = ☐   f) 72 – 5 = ☐

c) 19 – 10 = ☐   g) 50 – 5 = ☐

d) 24 – 5 = ☐

3. Dippy the Dragon had **45** tulips but she burned **10** of them with her breath.

How many tulips did Dippy have left?

Write the calculation here: ☐ – ☐ = ☐

Then her little brother ate **5** of the rest.

How many tulips did Dippy have left now?

Write the calculation here: ☐ – ☐ = ☐

TRY THIS Activity

Which parts of your body could you use to help you count in 5s and 10s? Did you know that frogs only have 4 fingers on each hand but 5 toes on each foot?

Check Your Progress!
Five Less And Ten Less ☐
Turn to page 48 and put a tick next to what you have just learned.

37

KS1: Adding & Taking Away

Top Tip! If your child struggles with anything, don't worry – let them go at their own pace.

Parents Start Here...

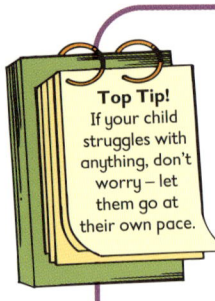

Question 3 is an example of the type of problem that your child will be beginning to tackle at school. The questions require that the child thinks about the problem, decides how to tackle it and then proceeds with the calculation.

Adding And Subtracting: Problems With Centimetres

Remember!

- We use centimetres and metres to measure length.
- There are 100 centimetres (cm) in a metre (m).
- You must remember to use the symbols cm and m.

1. Fill in the missing symbols:

a) 5 cm + 3 cm = 8 ☐

b) 12 cm – 4 ☐ = 8 cm

c) 18 m + 2 m = 20 ☐

2. This ruler is like a number line.

38

Adding And Subtracting: Problems With Centimetres

You can use it to answer these questions:

a) 4 cm + 5 cm = ☐ cm

b) 11 cm – 9 cm = ☐ cm

c) 9 cm + ☐ cm = 13 cm

d) 5 cm + 5 cm + 5 cm = ☐ cm

e) 2 cm + 3 cm + 4 cm = ☐ cm

3. Fodo the Frog is jumping across a pond by leaping on lily pads. The pond is 100 cm wide. Fodo has jumped 80 cm already. How much further does Fodo have to jump?

Put a tick next to the correct answer:

a) 100 cm ☐

b) 20 cm ☐

c) 80 cm ☐

TRY THIS Activity

Can you use a ruler to measure how long this book is?

Use a ruler to measure different things in your house.

Check Your Progress!

Adding And Subtracting: Problems With Centimetres ☐

Turn to page 48 and put a tick next to what you have just learned.

KS1: Adding & Taking Away

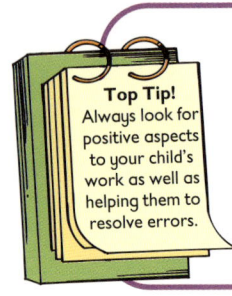

Top Tip! Always look for positive aspects to your child's work as well as helping them to resolve errors.

Parents Start Here...

The subject of time is also covered in the book **KS1 Revision, Practice & Home Learning: Shape, Size & Distance**.

Important Numbers To Know

Remember!
- We use numbers to tell us about lots of things.
- Time is measured using numbers.
- There are some important numbers we all need to know.

1. Complete the sentences using these numbers:

365   52   7   24   60   366   12

a) When I look at my watch I can count ☐ seconds in one minute.

b) There are ☐ days in one week.

c) There are ☐ days in one year, except in a Leap Year, when there are ☐.

d) Each year has ☐ weeks.

e) December is my favourite month. There are ☐ months in a year.

f) There are ☐ hours in one day.

40

Important Numbers To Know

2. Find out how many days there are in each month and complete these sentences:

January has ☐ days.

February has ☐ days, except in a Leap Year, when it has ☐ days.

March has ☐ days.

April has ☐ days.

May has ☐ days.

June has ☐ days.

July has ☐ days.

August has ☐ days.

September has ☐ days.

October has ☐ days.

November has ☐ days.

December has ☐ days.

TRY THIS Activity

Find out why we have Leap Years, and how often they occur.

Check Your Progress!
Important Numbers To Know ☐
Turn to page 48 and put a tick next to what you have just learned.

KS1: Adding & Taking Away

Top Tip! Try and incorporate what your child learns into everyday life – they will remember it even better.

Parents Start Here...

Ensure your child is able to write the names of all the numbers between one and ten. Help them learn the spellings of the next ten up to twenty.

Writing Numbers In Words

Remember!

- Numbers can be written as *digits*: 1, 2, 3, etc.
- Numbers can be written as *words*: one, two, three, etc.
- You need to know how to write numbers *both ways*.

1. Match the number to its name. One has been done for you:

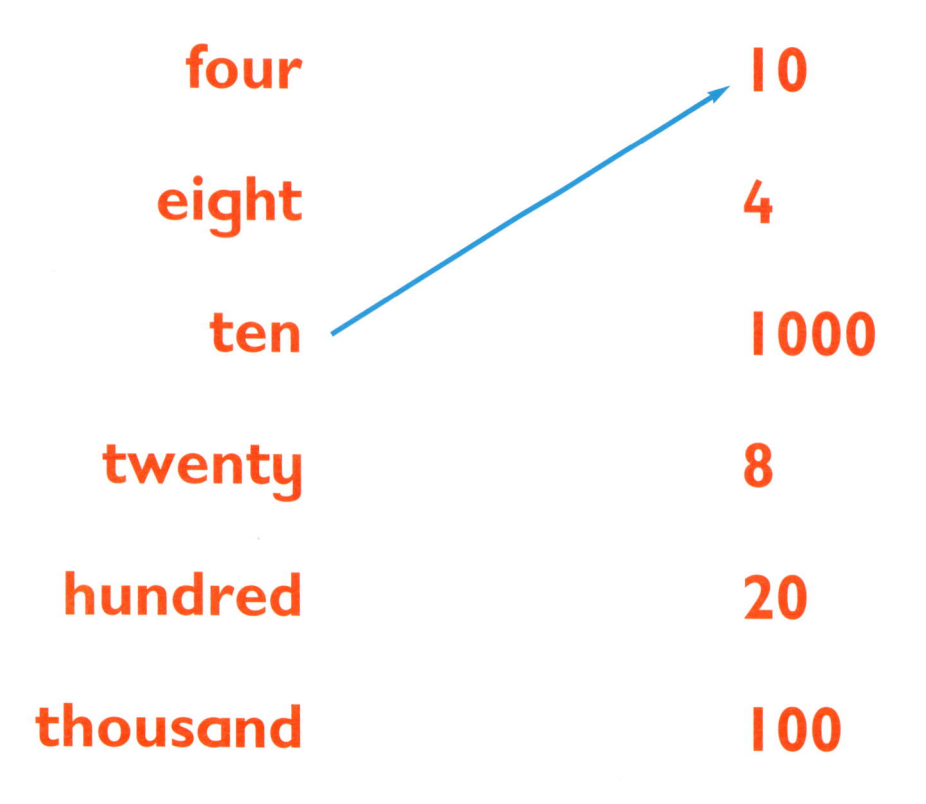

four	10
eight	4
ten	1000
twenty	8
hundred	20
thousand	100

Writing Numbers In Words

2. Write the name next to the number. Use a dictionary to help you:

a) 11

b) 12

c) 13

d) 14

e) 15

f) 16

g) 17

h) 18

i) 19

TRY THIS

Activity

If you find it hard to learn spellings, try writing each word out in big imaginary letters in the air. You could also write the names on to pieces of paper and stick them to your fridge.

Check Your Progress!
Writing Numbers In Words
Turn to page 48 and put a tick next to what you have just learned.

KS1: Adding & Taking Away

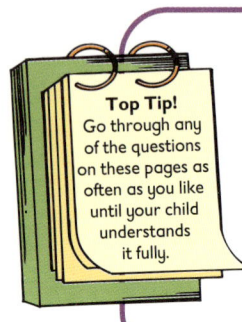

Top Tip! Go through any of the questions on these pages as often as you like until your child understands it fully.

Parents Start Here...

Aim to set your child 10 addition or subtraction sums every day. Repeat the same sums over and over and you will witness your child become very quick at simple mental maths.

Use Your Head!

Remember!

- Do as many sums as you can *in your head*.
- Is your answer a *sensible* one?
- Practising *number bonds* will help you do sums quickly.
- *Remember* the number patterns you have found.

Try to do as many of these sums and subtractions as you can in your head. Use the Number Square or make a number line if you get stuck:

1. Adding:

a) 5 + 5 =

b) 10 + 10 =

c) 10 + 15 =

d) 12 + 8 =

e) 13 + 7 =

f) 50 + 50 =

g) 2 + 8 =

h) 1 + 9 =

i) 16 + 4 =

j) 6 + 4 =

k) 40 + 10 =

l) 35 + 5 =

44

Use Your Head!

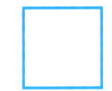

2. Subtracting:

a) 100 − 50 = ☐   g) 10 − 7 = ☐

b) 50 − 10 = ☐   h) 10 − 4 = ☐

c) 20 − 1 = ☐   i) 20 − 18 = ☐

d) 25 − 5 = ☐   j) 15 − 10 = ☐

e) 20 − 11 = ☐   k) 20 − 15 = ☐

f) 10 − 2 = ☐   l) 30 − 10 = ☐

TRY THIS

Activity

When you have finished these additions and subtractions you can put your pencil down, close the book, jump up and dance. Well done! Now it's time to play …

Check Your Progress!
                    Use Your Head! ☐
Turn to page 48 and put a tick next to what you have just learned.

45

KS1: Adding & Taking Away

Answers

Pages 4–5
1. 76
2. 26, 29
3. 10, 20, 30 etc
4. 17

Pages 6–7
1. 4 smiley faces
2. 3 sweets
3. 8 lollies
4. a) 12
   b) 14

Pages 8–9
1. 8, 11
2. a) 7
   b) 10
   c) 15
3. a) 8
   b) 11
   c) 16
4. 2, 4, 6, 8, 10, 12
5. 9, 11, 13, 15, 17, 19

Pages 10–11
1. 8
2. 9
3. 10
4. There are 3 groups of dots. Each group has 4 dots in it.

Pages 12–13
1. a) 2 has been added each time.
   b) These numbers are all even.
2. a) 3
   b) 18
3. a) 5
   b) 5
4. 4, 8, 12, 16, 20

Pages 14–15
1. 5
2. 2 more dots
3. 6
4. 7 + 3 = 10
   9 + 1 = 10
   4 + 6 = 10
   10 + 0 = 10
   2 + 8 = 10
   5 + 5 = 10

Pages 16–17
2 + 18 = 20
7 + 13 = 20
7 + 13 = 20
9 + 11 = 20
1 + 19 = 20
20 + 0 = 20
17 + 3 = 20
16 + 4 = 20
15 + 5 = 20
17 + 3 = 20
2 + 18 = 20
1 + 19 = 20
2 + 18 = 20
4 + 16 = 20
5 + 15 = 20
6 + 14 = 20
12 + 8 = 20
10 + 10 = 20

Pages 18–19
1. a) 4 bugs are left
   b) 7 – 4 = 3
2. a) 10 – 1 = 9
   b) 8 – 2 = 6
   c) 5 – 5 = 0
3. a) 5
   b) 4
   c) 8
   d) 7
   e) 9

Pages 20–21
1. a) 16
   b) 100
   c) 36
   d) 80
   e) 60
2. a) 75 – 2 = 73
   b) 13 – 1 = 12
   c) 40 – 2 = 38
   d) 28 – 2 = 26
   e) 88 – 2 = 86
3. a) 2
   b) 2
   c) 2
   d) 1

Pages 22–23
1. a) 30, 50, 80, 90
   b) 55, 75
   c) 33, 53, 83
   d) 29, 49, 69, 79
   e) 400, 600, 900
2. a) 0, 10, 100, 1000
   b) 4, 5, 50, 75, 91
   c) 74, 75, 82, 88, 91
3. Anything between 15 and 25 is a good estimate for Jar A and anything between 30 and 50 for Jar B.

Pages 24–25
1. 4
2. a) 8
   b) 12
3. a) 10
   b) 100
   c) 4
4. 20 → 10
   8 → 4
   14 → 7
   100 → 50

46

Answers

Pages 26–27
1. 32p
2. 8p
3. Three 10 pence coins
4. a) £1.00 or one pound
   b) £2.00 or two pounds

Pages 28–29
1. and 2.

5	10	15	20	25	30	35	40	45	50
55	60	65	70	75	80	85	90	95	100

Half the boxes are coloured.

3. a) 12 + 5 = 17
   b) 23 + 10 = 33
   c) 33 + 5 = 38
   d) 72 + 5 = 77
   e) 61 + 10 = 71
   f) 1 + 10 = 11
   g) 40 + 5 = 45
   h) 40 + 10 = 50
4. 10 + 15 = 25

Pages 30–31
1. 50
2. 80
3. a) 10 + 90 = 100
   b) 60 + 40 = 100
   c) 30 + 70 = 100
   d) 80 + 20 = 100
   e) 50 + 50 = 100
   f) 80 + 20 = 100
   g) 30 + 70 = 100
   h) 60 + 40 = 100
   i) 10 + 90 = 100

Pages 34–35
1. 54p
2. a) 65p
   b) 50p
   c) 5p
3. 40p
4. 50p
5. No. The jam tarts cost 20p.

Pages 36–37
1.

15 – 5 = 9	29 – 5 = 24	99 – 10 = 89	17 – 5 = 13
36 – 10 = 25	71 – 5 = 66	13 – 10 = 12	40 – 5 = 35
22 – 10 = 12	5 – 5 = 1	85 – 5 = 79	76 – 5 = 71

2. a) 60
   b) 90
   c) 9
   d) 19
   e) 89
   f) 67
   g) 45
3. 45 – 10 = 35
   35 – 5 = 30

Pages 38–39
1. a) cm
   b) cm
   c) m
2. a) 9
   b) 2
   c) 4
   d) 15
   e) 9
3. (b)

Pages 40–41
1. a) 60
   b) 7
   c) 365, 366
   d) 52
   e) 12
   f) 24
2. January, March, May, July, August, October and December all have 31 days. The rest have 30, except for February which has 28. In a Leap Year February has 29 days.

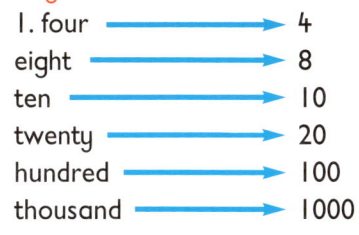

Pages 42–43
1. four → 4
   eight → 8
   ten → 10
   twenty → 20
   hundred → 100
   thousand → 1000

2. a) eleven
   b) twelve
   c) thirteen
   d) fourteen
   e) fifteen
   f) sixteen
   g) seventeen
   h) eighteen
   i) nineteen

Pages 44–45
1. a) 10
   b) 20
   c) 25
   d) 20
   e) 20
   f) 100
   g) 10
   h) 10
   i) 20
   j) 10
   k) 50
   l) 40
2. a) 50
   b) 40
   c) 19
   d) 20
   e) 9
   f) 8
   g) 3
   h) 6
   i) 2
   j) 5
   k) 5
   l) 20

47

Check Your Progress!

Check Your Progress!

Counting Numbers .... ☐

Adding One More And Two More .... ☐

Number Lines .... ☐

Counting In Groups .... ☐

Counting In Patterns .... ☐

Adding To Ten: Number Bonds .... ☐

Numbers To 20 .... ☐

Subtracting .... ☐

One Less And Two Less .... ☐

Bigger Numbers .... ☐

Doubling And Halving .... ☐

Addition: Money Problems .... ☐

Five More And Ten More .... ☐

Number Bonds To 100 .... ☐

Estimating .... ☐

Subtraction: Money Problems .... ☐

Five Less And Ten Less .... ☐

**Adding And Subtracting:
Problems With Centimetres** .... ☐

Important Numbers To Know .... ☐

Writing Numbers In Words .... ☐

Use Your Head! .... ☐

48